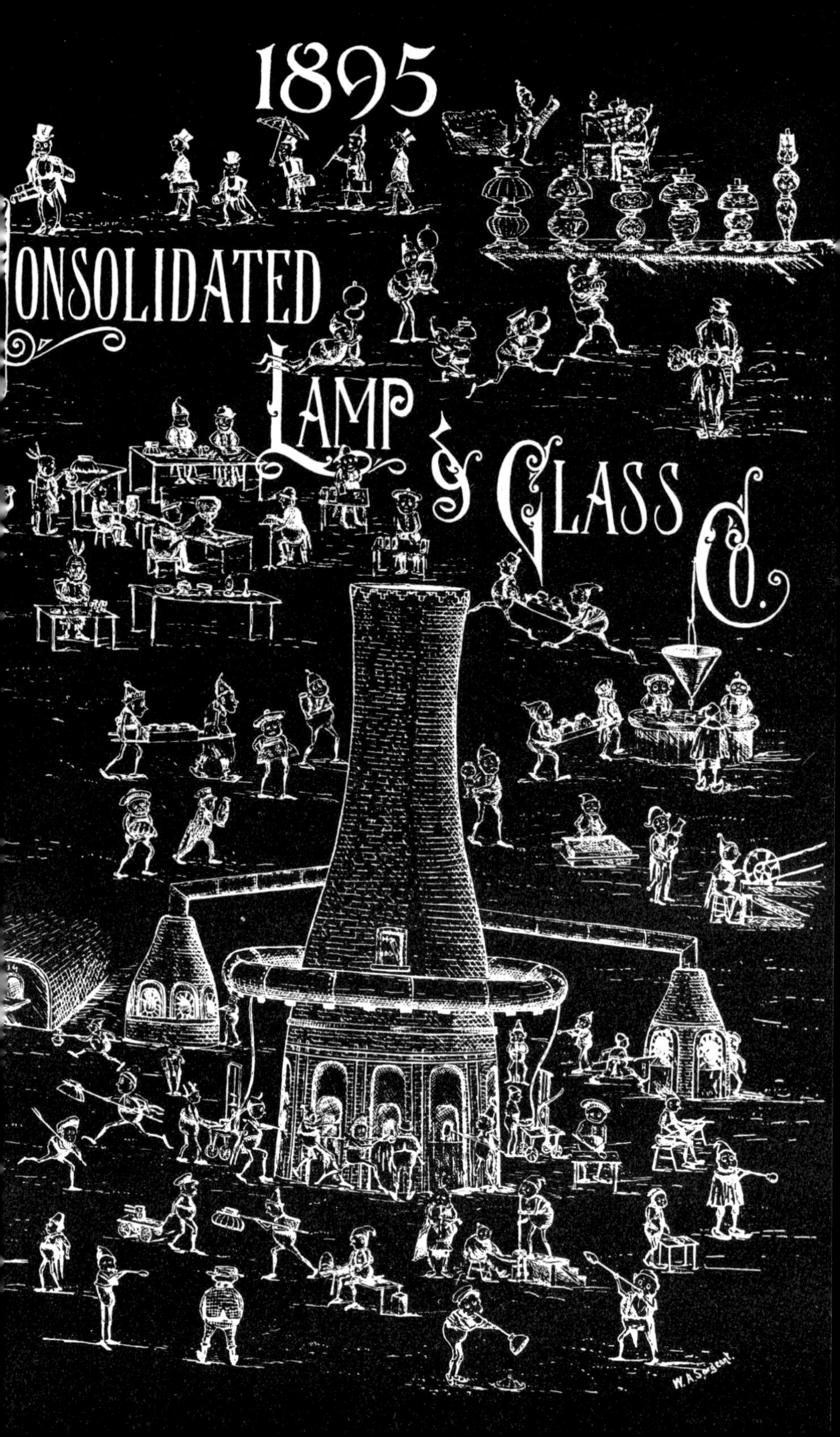
1895
ONSOLIDATED
LAMP
& GLASS
CO.
W. A. Sargent.

THE AUTHOR

Arthur Peterson was born in a homestead log cabin in the forest region of Minnesota in 1904, one of 14 children. He worked his way thru college, attaining five degrees, including a doctor of philosophy in economics and history at Harvard University.

A varied and progressive career of 38 years in the Federal Service entailed extensive foreign and domestic travel. Among other activities, he served as Secretary-Treasurer, and later President, of the Agricultural History Society; the first elected Chairman of the Advisory Council, Group Health Association, Washington, D .C.; and was one of the founders of the Economic History Association. He is listed in the International Who's Who of Intellectuals.

A yen for collecting led to a second and varied career, including research, lecturing, photography and writing on old glass. In this connection, 800 old glass salt shakers were given to the museum of the Minnesota Historical Society.

Dr. Peterson established an endowment for an annual historical essay contest in the Mora Public Schools, Mora, Minnesota; a trust for the Agricultural History Society to promote handicrafts among rural people; and a grant to the University of Florida for the first endowed public lectureship on death education in the United States. At 70, he founded the nonprofit Funeral Society of Mid-Florida for the promotion of simplicity and economy in funeral arrangements through advanced planning - and served as President thereof for five years.

400
TRADEMARKS
ON
GLASS

WITH ALPHABETICAL INDEX

By
ARTHUR G. PETERSON, Ph.D.

Author of *Glass Salt Shakers: 1,000 Patterns* and
Glass Patents and Patterns

PUBLISHED 1968
SECOND PRINTING 1969
THIRD PRINTING 1971
FOURTH PRINTING 1973
FIFTH PRINTING 1976
SIXTH PRINTING 1985 (REVISED)
SEVENTH PRINTING 1992

AVAILABLE FROM
L-W BOOK SALES
P.O. Box 69
Gas City, IN 46933

FOREWORD

Many people have the idea that trademarks on glass have been few and far between. Consequently, it probably will be a pleasant surprise to learn that over 200 companies in the United States have used 400 or more trademarks on blown, pressed, cut and engraved glass.

This definitive text will be of lasting interest and value to students of glassware. Glass collectors and dealers are fortunate that the necessary coincidences occurred to bring about such a document in this century rather than later. It required someone living near the Patent Office and the Library of Congress who had the time and ability as well as the motivation to undertake and complete a semi-charitable task.

Dr. Peterson has made a thorough and scholarly study of trademarks on glass and has summarized the information in concise and convenient form. Replicas of the original trademarks, from Patent Office records, are accompanied by the name and address of the owner, year of first use, and other information.

Frances Armentrout
President, Silver Spring, Maryland, Chapter,
National Early American Glass Club

ISBN: 0-9605664-1-4
Library of Congress Catalog Card Number 68-12557
© Arthur G. Peterson 1968

CONTENTS

The Author to the Reader

"Trademarks on Glass" was intended to be just another of my articles for HOBBIES Magazine. That was six years ago. Initial research in the United States Patent Office – a gold mine of information – made it evident that any quick treatment of trademarks could but skim the surface.

Trademarks have been the most neglected source of authentic and documented information for glass collectors and dealers. Official and private records provide a continuous and expanding flow of trademark information. Sooner or later some member of the glass collectors' fraternity will, I hope, enlarge upon my review of the first century of trademarks on glass.

I am indebted to Judge Arthur M. Smith, United States Court of Customs and Patent Appeals, and to Mr. John H. Merchant, United States Patent Office, for their review of the manuscript and helpful suggestions.

ARTHUR G. PETERSON

TRADEMARKS ON GLASS

Definition

A trademark, according to the Trademark Act of 1946, "includes any word, name, symbol, or device, or any combination thereof adopted and used by a manufacturer or merchant to identify his goods and to distinguish them from those manufactured or sold by others."

Scope of Survey and Report

This treatise covers 400 trademarks on glassware along with bits of information here and there. The major emphasis is on 355 trademarks in use before 1915 and registered in the United States Patent office. Thirty of these were registered by 25 European glass companies and 325 were registered by 195 American glass manufacturers and distributors. The other 45 or more consist of nonregistered marks and trademarks introduced after 1914.

Some cut-off date was desirable because of the long lag between first use and registration of some trademarks—over 50 years in two cases. Owing to this lag, all registrations of trademarks on glassware were examined through 1930 and a selective search was made from 1931 to 1967. The year 1914, which marks the beginning of World War I, seemed to be an appropriate cut-off for the present and upcoming generation of glass collectors. Nevertheless, considerable information is included about trademarks introduced since 1914.

Trademarks are included in this study only if they have been affixed or applied on the glass, not if they were listed for use only on stationery, packages and boxes. Trademarks specified for use only on watch crystals, electric light bulbs, window glass, plate and other flat and industrial glass also were excluded.

The use of trademarks on glassware in the United States as recorded in Patent Office records, began in a small way in the early 1860s. Consequently, this is mainly a record of trademarks used on glassware in the 55 years, 1860-1914, and registered at some time in the United States Patent Office. Many of these trademarks continued to be used after 1914 and a few of them are still in active use, but most of them have been abandoned. These trademarks are depicted by photographic copies of the drawings in the official records of the Patent Office, except 53 marks (words), which are shown in bold type.

The more pertinent information for collectors and dealers has been summarized from the official records to accompany the trademark illustrations. This includes the registrant's name and address, the year of first use, type of glassware, the more permanent methods of applying the trademark, and occasional annotations.[1]

---

[1] The first Federal Act relating to trademarks, July 8, 1870, was declared unconstitutional a decade later (100 USC 82). In applying it to intrastate commerce, Congress exceeded its authority to "regulate commerce with foreign nations, and among the several States, and with the Indian tribes . . ." Consequently, some trademarks registered since May 17, 1881, may have been used in intrastate commerce earlier than the recorded date of first use in interstate or foreign commerce.

In the case of old trademarks, the first use may have been by a predecessor of the listed registrant. A trademark may be transferred and its registration can be renewed as long as the mark is used in interstate or foreign commerce. In 1961, for example, the Cambridge Glass Co., Cambridge, Ohio, assigned all interest in four trademarks together with the good will of the business symbolized by said marks, to the Imperial Glass Corporation, Bellaire, Ohio. These were trademark words, with the year of first use as follows: **Cambridge Square,** 1952; **Rondo,** 1952; **Today,** 1956; **Wedding Rings,** 1955.

Information as to the method of applying the trademark to the glass became a victim of progress and was eliminated when the streamlined format for trademark specifications was adopted in 1954.

Value of Trademark Information

Collectors and dealers are becoming more knowledgeable about antiques and other collectables. Publications and even oral statements are being subjected to more critical reviews in glass clubs and other groups. Dissemination of information has become so widespread that finding a "sleeper" is almost a thing of the past. Collectors are becoming less gullible for heresay evidence and guesswork and are increasingly eager to separate facts from fancy.

Patents, registered trademarks, old catalogs and trade journals are the major primary sources of authentic, documentary information about old American glass. Trademarks on porcelains have been widely publicized, but little attention has been given to trademarks in books on glass.

Trademarks have several advantages over patents as a source of information for collectors. Federal law provides for continuous protection of a trademark by renewal of registration every 20 years, whereas design patents expire in 3½, 7 or 14 years, depending on the fee paid by the applicant, and patents on inventions expire in 17 years. There is no renewal provision for patents. Although trademarks may be pirated, this is less frequent than the copying or imitation of popular designs, even if still covered by a patent. Moreover, ownership and/or use of old molds for glassmaking have been transferred from one glass maker to another. Two major repositories of old and new molds long have been sources of many of our reproduction and reproduced pattern glass. Hence design patents or identification of the initial manufacturer may be of little value in determining the origin of a particular piece of glass.[2]

Trademarks are of special interest to collectors when they are used as permanent marks in the glass or other material. The chief value of such marks to the collector (as well as the producer) is to indicate origin, which in turn may be a useful guide to quality. A manufacturer or distributor who has a permanent mark in his wares is likely to have two things in which he takes pride: a good product and a good reputation.

Most trademark registrants (until 1954) listed several means by which their marks were put in or on the glass, such as: blown, burned, embossed, enameled, engraved, etched, impressed, incised, painted, or by use of a paper label.

---

[2] Copyrights of works of art executed in glass are also of some value in determining origin, but it is difficult to relate a given copyright to a particular glass object.

Collectors usually are interested in determining the age as well as the origin of their "treasures." Federal records of trademark registration specify a date when the mark was first used. This is of particular value in ascertaining the maximum age of the trademarked article and is noted here opposite the registrant's name.

If the use of a given trademark on some or all types of glass has been discontinued, it would be nice to ascertain the cut-off date for each type of glass. Such information, however, even if available, probably would be of limited value unless the mark was known to have been in continuous use on certain wares throughout the specified period. Discontinuing the use of a trademark may be a gradual and even an intermittent process. Moreover, if the registration has expired the trademark may be registered again under a new application.[3] Hence, a record of registry expirations would be of indeterminate value to collectors and might be misleading.

Trademarks pressed or blown in the glass at the time of its manufacture also have an advantage over signatures. Such trademarks are more standardized over time and cannot be added after the glass has cooled. Fraudulent signatures, on the other hand, can be (and have been) added to old glass. Etched marks, which are made with hydrofluoric acid, also can be added to cooled glass at any time.[4]

Registered trademarks have certain permanent or "essential features." Oftentimes there are some additional or non-essential features, which may be changed or omitted. Consequently, some variations in the appearance of a trademark may occur from time to time.

In the United States, Federal registration of trademarks began in 1870, whereas the first Federal patents and copyrights were granted in 1790, the first design patent in 1842, and the first plant patent in 1930.

Substantial changes in the trademark law occurred in 1881, 1905, 1920 and 1946. Under the Act of 1881, new registrations were good for 30 years. Since July 1905, new registrations have been good for 20 years and renewable every 20-year period thereafter, provided the mark still is used in interstate or foreign commerce, or provided there is a legitimate excuse for nonuse. Notice of registration may be given by displaying with the mark the letter R in a circle, or the words "Registered in the U.S. Patent Office," or "Reg. U.S. Pat.Off."

Rights in a trademark are acquired by use and are recognized at common law even if not registered. Without Federal registration, however, suit for restitution of a trademark cannot be brought in the Federal courts unless the controversy involves at least $10,000 and the parties reside in different States. In such case, the applicable state law governs the proceedings.

Many states have had provisions for registering trademarks. Before the development of modern transportation facilities and the accompanying expansion of interstate trade, state registration of trademarks on glass may have been worth while, but it would be of relatively little

---

[3] An "Index of Applicants" is maintained from January 1, 1922 to date.
[4] Fraudulent signatures are reviewed in **The Western Collector**, October 1967, pp. 7-11.
Ada Polak, in her book on Modern Glass, London, 1962, pp. 84-88, illustrated some 90 "signatures" in use on glass at that time, nearly all of which are of European origin.

value today. Glassware production in the United States has been largely in an approximate triangle from Maryland to Maine to Illinois, with increased concentration in the Ohio River Valley since 1889.

Search for Old Trademarks

A preliminary survey indicated that a comprehensive study of old trademarks on glass would require considerable time and resources. It turned out to be more of a one-man task than anticipated. In fact, the whole project came near being abandoned in its final stage owing to the high cost of photographing and reducing or enlarging each trademark individually.

Patent Office records are well classified and maintained to meet the needs of the patent and trademark system—primarily to meet the needs of industry and commerce. The records, however, are not designed to facilitate academic historical research and are not expected to be.

Many of the old trademark records are no longer extant, but an alphabetical microfilm record is available in the Search Room of Trademark Operations. The latter is a convenient record for ascertaining if a particular letter or word mark has been registered. The only complete historical record is in the large bound volumes in which trademark registrations are arranged chronologically. Separate annual indexes are available beginning 1881, but registrations prior to May 17, 1881 (Numbers 1-8190) are neither classified nor indexed in the Trademark Division of the Patent Office.

The limited official interest in these early trademark records is easy to justify. Although registration began in 1870, the termination in 1881 of all prior registrations made the earlier records unnecessary for administrative purposes. An historian, on the other hand, needs to survey such early records to satisfy his intellectual curiosity and to keep peace with his conscience.

Charles F. A. Hinrichs of New York, N. Y. obtained the first Patent-Office registration of a trademark for glassware. His trademark, No. 628 of January 2, 1872, portrays a bird (the fabled phoenix) along with the words "Fire-Proof Chimney," and was used as a label on lamp chimneys. The first registration of a trademark for glass tableware was obtained by Thomas G. Cook of Philadelphia, Pa., in the name of his company. His trademark, No. 1201 of April 8, 1873, consists of the word "CENTENNIAL" and was applied to glass vessels generally, while they were being "blown and molded or pressed."

A search was made of all files of abandoned, expired and active trademarks in Class 33 (glass). The classification categories include a wide range of animate as well as inanimate objects. The main classes are: arts and manufacturers, birds, buildings and scenery, designs, grotesque, human, invertebrate, (and vertebrate), letters, mammalia, mythology, portraits, slogans, statuary, and vegetation. Among the many subclasses are nests, rainbows, and spiderwebs.

As a double check, an examination was made of the annual indexes (which begin with 1881) to obtain a record of all trademarks listed under glass, lamps, bottles, etc. prior to 1931.

A special search was undertaken to find certain trademarks pictured by Dorothy Daniel in her book on *Cut and Engraved Glass,* Plates 164-165. Competent and accommodating officials in the Trademark Division concluded that there had been no Federal registration for most of these. Subsequent inquiry indicated that the source of these "missing" trademarks was "a page of reproductions of contemporary trademarks in a scrap book then in the Bella Landauer Collection at the New York Historical Society."[5]

Some of the early trademark illustrations in Patent-Office records are rather faded and the zerox copies purchased from the Patent Office in many cases required some art work to make them suitable for reproduction. Many were reordered several times when the original was known to be in good condition. Yet, about two percent of the illustrations obtained were so poor that they were excluded.

Most of the Patent-Office illustrations reproduced herein were reduced in size and a few were enlarged.

Classification of Information

Trademarks were separated into three groups in this study to facilitate reference by specialized collectors. Registrants, or assignees in a few cases, are listed alphabetically within each group.

Group I, for want of a better term, is labeled "tableware." It includes glassware in general, even some lamps, bottles, and jars if the registrant listed his trademark for use on all these articles. When a Group I trademark was specified for use also on lamps and/or bottles, for instance, such use is listed last in the right hand column to permit a quick reference by lamp and bottle collectors.

Group II trademarks were specified almost exclusively for use on lamps and lamp accessories such as chimneys, globes and shades. Only two manufacturers of these products also listed their trademark for use on bottles.

Group III trademarks were specified exclusively for bottles (including flasks), jars and other containers.

These groupings are based on information furnished in the application for registration of the trademark. No doubt some glass companies broadened or narrowed the field of use of a trademark from time to time and they probably made changes in the method of applying the trademark to the glass.

Historical Background

Applications for trademark registrations indicate that the use of trademarks on glassware in the United States began in 1860. A marked increase occurred in the 1870s, chiefly by lamp makers, followed by a sharp increase in the 1890s among all types of glass producers. The upward trend in use of trademarks, 1860-1914, is indicated in the accompanying table. These data, on the number of trademarks in use, do not reveal the full magnitude of trademark usage because of the growth in size and volume of output of most glass companies during the 55-year period from 1860 to 1914.

---

[5] Letter from Dorothy Daniel, Quitman, Georgia, to Arthur G. Peterson, November 29, 1963.

Trademarks in Use on Glassware, 1860-1914,

and

Registered in the United States Patent Office[1]

Period	Tableware[2]	Lamps and Accessories	Bottles and Jars	Total
1860-9	4	2	1	7
1870-9	8	18	6	32
1880-9	12	21	7	40
1890-9	29	47	20	96
1900-09	33	63	21	117
[3]1910-14	21	27	15	63
Total	107	[4]178	70	355

[1] Registration sometimes occurred soon after first use of the trademark whereas in many cases there was a lag of several years. In a few cases the lag in registration was from 25 to more than 50 years.

[2] Including ornamental and other household glass not elsewhere specified.

[3] Five-year totals lack comparability with earlier ten-year totals.

[4] Since 1914, relatively few trademarks have been introduced on lamps and lamp accessories, whereas many have been introduced on bottles, jars and other containers.

The number of glass houses in the United States more than doubled in the 20 years prior to 1880. By 1880 Pittsburgh, Pa. had become the world's center of the glass industry with over 30 glass houses. Census data on active glass houses in the United States indicate an increase from 169 in 1879 to a peak of 399 in 1904, with a decline to 348 in 1914. In 1879, Pennsylvania had 38 percent of our glass houses and West Virginia only 2 percent whereas the latter now is the leading state in glassware factories and production. The 169 active glass houses in 1879 were divided into four types by Warren Scoville in his classic on "Revolution in Glassmaking," as follows: pressed and blown glassware, 73; containers, 49; window glass, 42; plate glass, 5.

Data are not available on the volume of pressed and blown glassware produced, but census records reveal that the average value of production per firm more than doubled from 1879 to 1914. Time-series in terms of values normally include an element of price inflation. This historical phenomenon reflects the popularity of public spending and passing the debt on to succeeding generations. In the case of glassware, however, a notable deflation in prices occurred between 1860 and 1914. Thus, on a percentage basis, the increase in the total quantity of glass produced was much greater than the increase in its value from 1879-1914.

A marked decline in prices of glass tableware accompanied the shift from flint (leaded) glass to the new and improved soda-lime glass in the late 1860s and the 1870s. Various other factors contributed to lower per-unit production costs and wholesale prices of pressed and blown glassware to a record low in 1915.

Trademarks in Use on Glassware, 1860-1914,
and
Registered in the United States Patent Office

(Registration sometimes occurred soon after first use of the trademark whereas in many cases there was a lag of several years. In a few cases the lag in registration was from 25 to more than 50 years.)

GROUP I — Tableware

Trademark	Registrant	First used	Specified use and how applied
	Akro-Agate Co., Akron, Ohio and Clarksburg, W. Va. Succeeded by Masters Glass Co., Clarksburg, W. Va.	1911	Flower holders, ash trays, dishes and novelties, 1932 - 51. Pressed or label
	Anchor Glass Co., Mount Pleasant, Pa.	1907	Beer mugs, tea sets, tumblers, bottles and jars. Label
	La Compagnie Des Cristalleries De Baccarat, Meurthe, France	1860 (Reg. 1888)	Hollow glassware. "A decanter with a goblet and tumbler at opposite sides thereof." Printed or label
Baltimore Bargain House	Baltimore Bargain House, Baltimore, Maryland	1890	Cut and ornamental glass, tableware, bottles and jars
	Geo. Borgfeldt & Co., New York, N. Y.	1912	Cut glass. Label
NEARCUT	Cambridge Glass Co., Cambridge, Ohio A nonregistered trademark, consisting of a C in a triangle, was used beginning 1902.	1904	Tableware. Impressed or label

11

Trademark	Registrant	First used	Specified use and how applied
PURO (logo)	Centadrink Filters Co. Inc., New York, N.Y.	1913	Goblets, tumblers, carafes and siphon-bottles. Blown or label
Century (logo)	Century Inkstand Co., New York, N. Y.	1893	Inkstands. Stamped
(globe logo)	E. De La Chapelle & A.M. Paturle, Brooklyn, N.Y. Succeeded by E. De La Chapelle & Co., Ottawa, Ill., and later by La Bastie, Glass Co., Ottawa, Illinois	1876	All types of glassware. By 1906, this trademark apparently was used only on lamp chimneys. Blown or ground
LA BASTIE	E. De La Chapelle & A. M. Paturle, Brooklyn, N.Y. By 1915 this trademark had passed to Macbeth-Evans Glass Co. and was used only on lamp glasses and lamp globes	1876	All types of glassware. Etched or impressed
(leaf logo)	T. B. Clark & Co., Seelyville, Pa.	1898	Artistic cut glassware. Stamped
COHANSEY	Cohansey Glass Mfg. Co., Bridgeton, N.J.	1870	Window glass and other glass articles
CENTENNIAL.	T. G. Cook & Co., Philadelphia, Pa. First trademark registered in U. S. for use on glass tableware	1873	"Pressed, cut, molded or blown" glassware. Blown or molded
(Corning logo)	Corning Glass Works, Corning, N.Y. (See Steuben)	1878	Essential feature is "Corning." Blown or label

Trademark	Registrant	First used	Specified use and how applied
	Corning Glass Works, Corning, N.Y. Early use was on lamp glasses and globes by Macbeth Evans Glass Co. and predecessors. A similar silhouette mark was introduced in 1940.	1880	Man with blowpipe. Etched or on label
	Corning Glass Works, Corning, N.Y.	1904	Cut glass and artistic glassware. Impressed or on label
	Corning Glass Works, Corning, N.Y.	1904	Cut glass and artistic glassware. Impressed or on label
	Corning Glass Works, Corning, N.Y. Corning Glass Works also registered five names as trademarks for glass with the year of first use as follows: NONEX, 1909; NOVIL, NULTRA, RESISTAL, and ULTRA, in 1914.	1909	Glass. Impressed or label
	Corona Cut Glass Co., Toledo, Ohio	1906	Cut and engraved glassware. Label
	Daudt Glass & Crockery Co., Toledo, Ohio	1909	Fancy and ornamental glassware for table service. Etched
BEAUMIROIR.	Charles T. DeForest, New York, N.Y.	1884	Decorative glass. Engraved or printed

Trademark	Registrant	First used	Specified use and how applied
	E. D. Dithridge, Allegheny, Pa.	1877	A portrait of the late Edward Dithridge. Glass in general, including lamps
COLONIAL	C. Dorflinger & Sons, White Mills, Pa.	1892	Cut glass.* Label cut, engraved or blown
LORRAINE	C. Dorflinger & Sons, White Mills, Pa.	1894	Cut glass.* Label, cut, engraved or blown
TERU-TERU	Thomas Drysdale & Co., New York, N.Y.	1886	Glassware, other household articles, and lamps. Stamped
	Dominique Durand, New York, N.Y.	1875	Glass silvered by Durand's patented process. Printed
ATHOSGLASS	Duryea & Potter, New York, N.Y.	1901	Mosaic and decorative glass. Essential feature is "ATHOS." Blown or stenciled.
	O. F. Egginton Co., Corning, N.Y.	1899	Cut glassware. Engraving or etching.
FOSTORIA	Fostoria Glass Co., Moundsville, W.Va.	1891 (Reg. 1927)	Tableware. Label

* Perhaps used on Steuben-type colored art glass, 1916-1921.

Trademark	Registrant	First used	Specified use and how applied
	Fostoria Glass Co., Moundsville, W.Va.	1909	Tableware. Label
IRIS	Fostoria Glass Specialty Co., Fostoria, Ohio Trademark assigned in 1910 to General Electric Co. of N.Y.	1910	Glass in general, including illuminating glassware and bottles. Impressed
Japana	M. V. Garnsey, Spring Lake and Grand Haven, Mich.	1906	Glass vases, flower-holders and statuettes. Molded
C F H GDM	E. Gerard, Dufraisseix & Morel, Limoges, France	1882	Glass, porcelain, crockery and earthenware. Stamped
FRANKLIN	Gillinder & Sons, Philadelphia, Pa. and its predecessor, the Franklin Flint Glass Works	1860 (Reg. 1914)	Glass in general, including illuminating glassware. Etched
	Gillinder & Sons, Philadelphia, Pa.	1874	Label for glassware, including lamps, etc. Essential features are "G & S" and the faint circle
GILLINDER	Gillinder & Sons, Philadelphia, Pa.	1883	Etched on glass articles, including lamps, etc.
	T. G. Hawkes & Co., Corning, N.Y.	1890	Cut glass and engraved glass. Two hawkes in lower two-thirds of a trefoiled ring. Engraved or label
	T. G. Hawkes & Co., Corning, N.Y.	1890 (Reg. 1926)	Cut glass and engraved glass. Two hawkes in lower two-thirds of a trefoiled ring. Engraved or label

15

Trademark	Registrant	First used	Specified use and how applied
GRAVIC	T. G. Hawkes & Co., Corning, N.Y.	1902	Cut glass and engraved glass. Engraved or label
(diamond with H)	A. H. Heisey & Co., Newark, Ohio	1900	Pressed glassware. Pressed
(diamond) PLUNGER CUT	A. H. Heisey & Co., Newark, Ohio	1900	Pressed glassware. Pressed
	A. H. Heisey & Co., Newark, Ohio	1905	Pressed or b l o w n glassware. Pressed, blown or label
(triangle with pitcher) (triangle with shaker)	A. H. Heisey & Co., Newark, Ohio Two later Heisey trademarks are: An oval, usually in blue, first used in 1916; also the word Heisey above an H in a diamond, all enclosed within a double border. The latter was first used in 1932 and was acquired by the Imperial Glass Co., May 1, 1958.	1908	Molasses jugs and condiment shakers. Label
(circle J. HOARE & CO. 1853)	J. Hoare & Co., Corning, N.Y. The company traced its origin to 1853.	1895	C u t a n d engraved glass. Essential features are the two circles and the 1853. Etched
(NUCUT)	Imperial Glass Co., Bellaire, Ohio	1911	Pressed and blown glass. Stamped or impressed

Trademark	Registrant	First used	Specified use and how applied
IM PE RI AL	Imperial Glass Co., Bellaire, Ohio In 1939, a new trademark was introduced in which the word Imperial was combined with a sketch of a tilted drinking vessel.	1913	T a b l e w a r e. Impressed
(arrows cross symbol)	Imperial Glass Co., Bellaire, Ohio	1913	T a b l e w a r e. Impressed
(cross symbol)	Imperial Glass Co., Bellaire, Ohio The Imperial Glass Co. registered no less than 17 trademarks between 1940 and 1963. Among these were **"Cape Cod,"** first used in 1932, and the well-known I and G, superimposed, first used in 1951. See n o t a t i o n under A. H. Heisey & Co.	1914	Tableware. Pressed or blown
CHIPPENDALE	Jefferson Glass Co., Follansbee, W.Va.	1907	Tableware and ornamental glass. Label
(oval AMBERINA N.E.G.W.)	Edward D. Libbey, Boston, Mass. For W. L. Libbey & Son, Cambridge, Mass.	1882	A m b e r i n a was a newly-coined w o r d. Label
Libbey	Libbey Glass Co., Toledo, Ohio	1895	Cut glass. Etched
Libbey	Libbey Glass Co., Toledo, Ohio	1896	Cut & etched glass. Etched or label
Libbey	Libbey Glass Co., Toledo, Ohio	1901	Cut glass and electric light g l o b e s. Etched
(star in circle)	Libbey Glass Co., Toledo, Ohio A number of later "Libbey" trademarks were used on various drinking vessels, bowls, etc.:	1901	Shaped blanks intended for cut-glass articles. Stamped or etched

17

Trademark	Registrant	First used	Specified use and how applied
	(a) The word "Libbey" in a double circle was first used in 1924. (b) The words "Libbey CRYSTAL" in a circle were registered by The Libbey Glass Manufacturing Co.; used beginning June 1933, and later allowed to expire. (c) The words "Libbey Safedge" in a broken circle were registered by Owens-Illinois Glass Co. in 1949, but had been used since September 1933. A similar trademark with the words "Libbey PRESSED" was used on "bottles and jars made of glass" for a limited time beginning August 1947. (Trademarks are numbered by the U. S. Patent Office according to the date of registration, not the date when first used).		
	Lotus Cut Glass Co., Barnesville, Ohio	1911	Cut glass. Label
PRESCUT	McKee-Jeannette Glass Works, Jeannette, Pa.	1903	Tableware. Impressed or label
	Franz A. Mehlem, Bonn, Germany	1890	Glass and crockery. Essential features are the crown and the monogram "FAM" on a scroll. Impressed or embossed
WAVE CREST WARE	C. F. Monroe Co., Meriden, Conn.	1892	"Opal glassware." Only the words "Wave Crest" are essential features
KELVA	C. F. Monroe Co., Meriden, Conn.	1904	"Opal glassware"

18

Trademark	Registrant	First used	Specified use and how applied
	Mount Washington Glass Co., New Bedford, Mass. (See Shirley, Frederick S.)	1892	Tableware and fancy articles. RF, with the R in reverse. In or on the glass
	Mount Washington Glass Co., New Bedford, Mass. (See Shirley, Frederick S.)	1892	Tableware and fancy articles. CM as a monogram arranged with a crown (Crown Milano). In or on the glass
KOH-I-NOOR	Richard Murr, San Francisco, Calif.	1905	Cut glass. Label
	Nelson Glass Co., Muncie, Indiana	1891	Tableware receptacles, bottles and jars. Essential feature is "SAFETY." Blown or label
COMMUNITY	Oneida Community, Ltd., Oneida, N.Y.	1914	Glass bowls, plates, pitchers, platters, nappies, vases and jars. Stamped or printed
OVINGTON'S	Ovington Bros. Co., New York, N.Y. Renewed to the Ovington Gift Shop in 1942.	1895	Glass tableware, bowls, boxes, trays, vases and jars. Label
	Austin D. Palmer, Coshocton, Ohio	1892	Glass paperweights and calendars. Essential feature is "World's Fair." Blown or printed
	Passow & Sons, Chicago, Illinois	1914	Hollow ware, drinking vessels and bottles. Label
ROYAL BRAND	H. Perilstein, Philadelphia, Pa.	1906	Cut, ornamental and industrial glass. Label

Trademark	Registrant	First used	Specified use and how applied
	Phoenix Glass Co., Monaca, Pa. and Pittsburgh, Pa.	1881	Ornamental glass, tableware, lamps, etc. Engraved or etched
	Pilkington Bros. Limited, St. Helens, England and later by Pilkington Glass Mfg. Co., Toronto, Canada	1877	Ornamental, cathedral and other glass. Printed or impressed
UNION A F MADE	Edward A. Power & Co., Pittsburgh, Pa.	1897	Essential feature is "AF." Pressed or blown
Quezal	Quezal Art Glass and Decorating Co., New York, N.Y.	1901	Goblets, vases, plaques and mantel ornaments. Ground or label
	Reid Bros., San Francisco, Calif. and Seattle, Washington	1909	Cups, tubes, bottles and jars. Stamped or label
REGAL BRAND	Royal Glass Co., Centralia, Illinois	1910	Enameled, window and other glass. Label
	C. F. Rumpp & Sons, Inc., Philadelphia, Pa.	1892	Glassware, et al. Impressed or label

Trademark	Registrant	First used	Specified use and how applied
	Schott & Gen, Jena, Germany	1897	Glassware. Trademark "usually is burned in"
	Schott & Gen, Jena, Germany	1904	Glass plates, tubes, laboratory vessels and "lamp-glasses." Burned or label
	Schott & Gen, Jena, Germany	1905	Glass plates, tubes, laboratory vessels and "lamp-glasses." Burned or label
	Frederick S. Shirley, New Bedford, Mass. The Russian eagle later was adopted for use in a trademark of the Mount Washington Glass Co.	1882	Glass tableware and fancy glass articles. Only essential feature is "Russian." Label
	Frederick S. Shirley, New Bedford, Mass.	1884	''Glass tableware and fancy glass articles having colors shading into each other.'' Essential feature is "Rose." Illustration has "Rose Amber" and "Mt. W.G.Co." Label
	Frederick S. Shirley, New Bedford, Mass.	1885	Glass tableware and fancy glass articles. Only essential feature is "Peach." Impressed or label

Trademark	Registrant	First used	Specified use and how applied
SILEX	Silex Co., Malden, Mass., Assignee from Hazel Bridges. Silex was registered as Trademark No. 3,437 in 1876 by Huwer & Dannenhoffer, Brooklyn, N.Y., and used as a trademark for lamp chimneys as early as 1870, but only on packages and for advertising.	1913	Glassware. B l o w n, engraved or label
	Solar Prism Co., Cleveland, Ohio	1899	Glass tiles, et al
AURENE	Steuben Glass Works, Corning, New York Registered to the Corning Glass Works in 1924.	1904	Vases, bowls, compotes, j u g s a n d d i s h e s. Cut, engraved or label
	Manufactures Des Glaces et Products Chimiques de ST. GOBAIN, Chauny & Cirey, Paris, France	1895	Glassware and plate glass. Printed, impressed or label
	L. Straus & Sons, New York, N.Y.	1894	Cut glass. On glass or label
	Thatcher Bros., Fairhaven, Mass.	1894	Cut glass. Label
TIFFANY	Tiffany & Company, New York, N.Y.	1868 (Reg. 1920)	"Table glassware." Stamping
TIFFANY&CO.	Tiffany & Company, New York, N.Y.	1868 (Reg. 1920)	"Table glassware." Stamping
	Tiffany Frances, Hoboken, N.J. and Corona, N.Y. (Louis C. Tiffany, Pres.)	1902	Decorative glass, enamels and pottery. "LCT" in the form of a m o n o g r a m. Printed, branded or label

Trademark	Registrant	First used	Specified use and how applied
	Tiffany Glass and Decorating Co., Jersey City, N.J. & New York, N.Y. Inserted between the words "Favrile" and "Glass" may be a word descriptive of particular kinds of glass such as "Fabric," "Sunset," "Horizon," "Twig," "Lace," etc.	1892	Decorative glass. Essential features are the monogram of "T G D Co." and "Favrile." Branded
	Tiffany Studios, New York, N.Y.	1905 (Reg. 1930)	Glass vases, bowls, compotes, d i s h e s , drinking vessels and l a m p s h a d e s . Stamped, etched, engraved or label
GLOBE 	William J. Tweed, Milville, N.J.	1904	G r a d u a t e d glassware
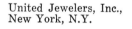HALLMARK	United Jewelers, Inc., New York, N.Y.	1914	Glassware. Etched
	United States Glass Co., Pittsburgh, Pa. A non-registered trademark consisting of the letters U and S, superimposed, were embossed on some pattern glass such as the Athenia (Panelled 44), introduced in 1912.	1911	"Table-glass." Label
	Weiss & Biheller, Ltd., London, England	1906	H o l l o w tableware. Impressed or label
VERKO	Florence Talbot Westbrook, San Francisco, Calif.	1912	Hand-painted glassware. Label

Trademark	Registrant	First used	Specified use and how applied
	Westmoreland Glass Co., Grapeville, Pa. This mark along with "authentic milk glass" was first used in 1940.	1910	Tableware. Label
	Westmoreland Specialty Co., Grapeville, Pa.	1910	Pressed glassware. Pressed
	C. E. Wheelock & Co., Peoria, Illinois	1898	Cut glass. Stenciled, printed or label
	Thomas Wightman, Pittsburgh, Pa.	1894	"T W G Co." in a monogram. Stenciled
	Wolf & Gross, New York, N.Y.	1893	"Hollow glass tableware." A woman performing a skirt dance. Enameled or label

Trademark	Registrant	First used	The more permanent types of the mark
AUTOLYTE	Frederic E. Baldwin, New York, N.Y.	1900	Stamped or printed
Boulevard	J. W. Bartlett, New York, N.Y.	1871	Blown, molded, cut, or ground
SILVER	La Bastie Glass Co., Ottawa, Illinois	1896	Blown or ground
	Best Light Co., Canton, Ohio	1895	Label
	Geo. Borgfeldt & Co., New York, N.Y.	1913	Imprinted
"SEARCH-LIGHT"	Bridgeport Brass Co., Bridgeport, Conn.	1894	Imprinted or embossed
BLUE RIBBON	Buckley-Newhall Co., New York and Brooklyn, N.Y.	1910	Label
	Buckley-Newhall Co., New York and Brooklyn, N.Y.	1910	Label
BANNER.	Frederick W. Buning, New York, N.Y.	1893	Engraved
	Chandler Specialty Mfg. Co., Boston, Mass.	1902	Label
BURGLAR'S HORROR.	Clarkes-Pyramid and Fairy Light Co., Limited, London, England	1884	Stamped
	Clarkes-Pyramid and Fairy Light Co., Limited, London, England	1891	Applied to lamps in their mfg., and to oil-bottles with a label

Trademark	Registrant	First used	The more permanent types of the mark
CRICKLITE	Clarkes-Pyramid and Fairy Light Co., Limited, London, England	1894	Stamped
Coleman Quick-Lite	Coleman Lamp Co., Wichita, Kansas	1913	"Applied directly to the goods"
DEGEA	Deutsche Gasgluhlicht Actien Gesellschaft, Berlin, Germany	1902	Stamped or burned on
BRIGHT STAR	Lewis P. Dexter, New York, N.Y.	1904	Impressed
A N? ı	R. E. Dietz Co., New York, N.Y.	1874	Stamped or impressed
N? 74	R. E. Dietz Co., New York, N.Y.	1875	Stamped or impressed
	R. E. Dietz Co., New York, N.Y. The R. E. Dietz Co. also registered 17 names as trademarks with the year of first use as follows: CORPORATION, 1886; BOY, ROCKET, and U.S. in 1892; ROYAL, 1895; LUNA, 1898; IDEAL and REGAL in 1902; DAINTY and VESTA, in 1904; ACME, BLIZZARD, JUNIOR, PIONEER, and VULCAN, in 1906; LITTLE GIANT, 1907; and LITTLE WIZZARD, 1914.	1891	Label
	Dithridge & Co., Pittsburgh, Pa.	1896	Label
	Richard Douglas & Co., New York, N.Y. Below the rooster are the words, "Lucidus est Vestigia."	1871	Label

Trademark	Registrant	First used	The more permanent types of the mark
	Richard Douglas & Co., New York, N.Y.	1874	Label
	Richard Douglas & Co., New York, N.Y.	1877	Blown
E. & J.	Edmunds & Jones Mfg. Co., Detroit, Michigan	1904	Stamped
	Ehrich & Graetz, Berlin, Germany	1886	Impressed or etched
Graetzin	Ehrich & Graetz, Berlin, Germany	1900	Stamped
 NOBLAC	Fostoria Glass Specialty Co., Fostoria, Ohio and Jersey City, N.J.	1904	Etched
NOREC	Fostoria Glass Specialty Co., Fostoria, Ohio and Jersey City, N.J.	1905	Stamped or printed
ACORN	Fostoria Glass Specialty Co., Fostoria, Ohio and Jersey City, N.J.	1908	Label
	Fostoria Glass Specialty Co., Fostoria, Ohio and Jersey City, N.J. Assigned to the General Electric Co.	1911	Label
	Oscar O. Friedlaender and predecessors, New York, N.Y. The word "Fireproof," or "Indifferent" appears below the lion on the earlier goods.	1898	Etched

Trademark	Registrant	First used	The more permanent types of the mark
GENERAL	General Automobile Supply Co., New York, N.Y.	1905	Stamped
SUDAN	General Electric Co., Schenectady, N.Y.	1913	Impressed
White Star	Gill Brothers Co., Steubenville, Ohio	1884	All these trademarks by Gill Brothers Co. were etched on the glass, or printed on a label attached to the article
BESSEMER	Gill Brothers Co., Steubenville, Ohio	1885	
SAMSON	Gill Brothers Co., Steubenville, Ohio	1887	
WARRANTED BEST LEAD FLINT / OIL FINISHED FIRE PROOF	Gill Brothers Co., Steubenville, Ohio	1890	
HAMMER	Gill Brothers Co., Steubenville, Ohio	1896	
MONARCH	Gill Brothers Co., Steubenville, Ohio	1897	

Trademark	Registrant	First used	The more permanent types of the mark
	Gill Brothers Co., Steubenville, Ohio	1900	
	Gill Brothers Co., Steubenville, Ohio	1901	
FINE ANCO FLINT	Gill Brothers Co., Steubenville, Ohio	1901	
GOOD LUCK	Gill Brothers Co., Steubenville, Ohio	1907	
	Gill Brothers Co., Steubenville, Ohio	1908	
UNICORN	Gill Brothers Co., Steubenville, Ohio The Gill Brothers Co. also registered ten names as trademarks with the year of first use as follows: SAMPSON, 1887; GRANITE, 1890; VICTOR TOP and OK, 1898; CORONET, 1900; ROCK, 1901; LUCKY CROSS, 1908; PARIAN and ACMELITE, 1911; and GLORIA, 1912.	1911	
	Gillinder & Sons, Inc., Philadelphia, Pa. and its predecessor, the Franklin Flint Glass Works	1860 (Reg. 1907)	Vignette of Benjamin Franklin, which, in some cases was enclosed in a square along with "Lead Glass, Guaranteed, G & S." Label (See *Milk Glass*, Belknap, plate 188)

29

	Gillinder & Sons, Inc., Philadelphia, Pa.	1907	Label
MICRA	Gillinder & Sons, Inc., Philadelphia, Pa.	1911	Label
NEBULITE	Gillinder & Sons, Inc., Philadelphia, Pa.	1911	Etched
POLYCASE	Gleason-Tiebout Glass Co., New York, N.Y.	1910	Impressed
Gral	Gruder, Blank & Co. M.B.H., Berlin, Germany	1903	Stamped or printed
C.T.HAM MFGCoNo 6 Square Lamp	C. T. Ham Manufacturing Co., Rochester, N.Y. This company also registered six other trademarks and noted the first year of use as follows: NO. 7, NO. 8, NO. 9 and NO. 10, in 1887; HAM'S, 1890; and NO. 40, in 1904.	1887	Stenciled
OLD SOL	Hawthorne Manufacturing Co., Bridgeport, Conn.	1910	Impressed or stamped
SUN-FLASH	Alexander Hemsley Philadelphia, Pa.	1892	Stamped or stenciled
KLEEMANN	Charles F. A. Hinrichs, New York, N.Y. Carl A. Kleeman of Erfurt, Prussia, produced Kleeman or German Student Lamps. After his death in 1871, Hinrichs — his exclusive U.S. agent since 1863—obtained the registered "Kleeman" trademark.	1863	Stamped
	Charles F. A. Hinrichs, New York, N.Y. This phoenix, along with the words "Fire-Proof Chimney," is the first trademark for glassware registered in United States. (Jan. 9, 1872)	1871	Label
PETROLITE	George H. Holgate, Philadelphia, Pa.	1905	Blown or molded

Trademark	Registrant	First used	The more permanent types of the mark
	Holophane Glass Co., New York, N.Y. The Holophane Glass Co. also registered six trademark names, first used in 1908, which were pressed in the glass or placed thereon with a paper label, namely: **FLECFRAC, LUNAR, POLAR, PRISMOLIER, RAZLDAZL,** and **SATIN FINISH.**	1900	Etched or pressed
AIR·O·LITE	Hydro Carbon Co., Wichita, Kansas	1911	Label
ISCO	International Shade Co., Springfield, Mass.	1912	Label
	K. E. Jacobson & E. H. Fessenden, Brooklyn, N.Y.	1888	S t a m p e d or imprinted
LUCEo	Jefferson Glass Co., Follansbee, W.Va.	1910	Label
	Jefferson Glass Co., Follansbee, W.Va.	1913	Impressed
ANNEALED FLINT GLASS J.M?D & S. BOSTON	Jones, McDuffee & Stratton Boston, Mass.	1877	Label
CUNARD FIRE TESTED	Jones, McDuffee & Stratton Boston, Mass.	1880	Label

Trademark	Registrant	First used	The more permanent types of the mark
JUSTRITE	Justrite Manufacturing Co., Chicago, Illinois	1911	Stenciled or stamped
	Kauffeld Glass Co., Matthews, Indiana	1902	"Labels and acids"
"Superlux"	Lighting Studios Co., New York, N.Y.	1913	Burned
REGAL	Lippincott Glass Co., Cincinnati, Ohio and Alexandria, Indiana	1896	Etched
Spookie Shades	Livermore & Knight Co., Providence, R.I.	1907	Label
OIL GUARD LAMP.	George H. Lomax, Somerville, Mass.	1871	Stamped or cast
HITCHCOCK	F. H. Lovell & Co., Arlington, N.J.	1873	Die-stamping
The Auto Supply Co.	John Lurie, 1733 Broadway, New York, N.Y.	1905	Label
	Macbeth-Evans Glass Co., Pittsburgh, Pa. and its predecessors, E. De La Chapelle & Co., and the La Bastie Glass Co.	1880	Etched
	Macbeth-Evans Glass Co., Pittsburgh, Pa. and predecessors Originally owned by Hogan Evans & Co., Pittsburgh, Pa.	1883	Etched

Trademark	Registrant	First used	The more permanent types of the mark
	Macbeth-Evans Glass Co., Pittsburgh, Pa. and predecessors	1884	Etched
	Macbeth-Evans Glass Co., Pittsburgh, Pa. and predecessors	1892	Etched
	Macbeth-Evans Glass Co., Pittsburgh, Pa. and predecessors	1894	Etched
	Macbeth-Evans Glass Co., Pittsburgh, Pa. and predecessors	1894	Etched
	Macbeth-Evans Glass Co., Pittsburgh, Pa. and predecessors	1895	Etched
	Macbeth-Evans Glass Co., Pittsburgh, Pa. and predecessors The Macbeth-Evans Glass Co. also registered nine names as trademarks with the year of first use as follows: **CRUCIBLE**, 1893; **ATLAS**, 1894; **TECO**, 1897; **CRESCENT**, 1898; **SUNSET**, 1899; **PARAGON**, 1900; **ALBA**, 1902; **ADMANT**, 1903; and **THERMO**, 1905 (later acquired by Corning Glass Works).	1897	Etched
	McFaddin & Co., New York, N.Y.	1909	Embossed or molded
	McKee & Brothers, Pittsburgh, Pa.	1890	Label

Trademark	Registrant	First used	The more permanent types of the mark
MILLER	Edward Miller & Co., Meriden, Conn.	1893	Label and other means
	Minneapolis Glass Co., Minneapolis, Minn.	1888	Label
MOONLIGHT.	Moonlight Patent Lamp Co., Ltd., Liverpool, England	1894	Stamped
	Moritz Kirchberger, New York, N.Y.	1898	Imprinted
	Moritz Kirchberger, New York, N.Y.	1903	Imprinted
	Mount Washington Glass Works, New Bedford, Mass.	1874	Label
	Otis A. Mygatt, New York, N.Y.	1901	Etched
NULITE	National Stamping & Electric Works, Chicago, Ill.	1908	Stamped

Trademark	Registrant	First used	The more permanent types of the mark
STORM KING	National Stamping & Electric Works, Chicago, Ill.	1914	Stamped
Three Feather Brand	Wm. R. Noe, New York, N.Y.	1895	Etched or engraved
	Pabst & Arming, New York, N.Y.	1879	Molded or branded
	Pabst & Esch, New York, N.Y.	1875	Label
	Packard Motor Car Co., Detroit, Michigan	1908	Affixed on a metal plate
	S. J. Pardessus & Co., New York, N.Y. Between the two oval lines are the words, "Cylindres, Cristal, Qualite, Superieure."	1873	Not specified
ORIGINAL TT	Parker & Sanders, Birmingham, England	1893	Impressed or stamped

Trademark	Registrant	First used	The more permanent types of the mark
FINE FLINT TIGER BRAND OIL FINISHED	Peerless Lead Glass Works, Ellwood City, Pa. The word Peerless in a formee cross was used as early as 1891.	1896	Label
VOLLENDEN * PHOENIX * WARE	Phoenix Glass Co., Pittsburgh, Pa.	1896	Engraved
FAIRY.	Price's Patent Candle Co. Ltd., London, Battersea and Cheshire, England	1884	Label
	Gebr. Putzler Glashutten-Werke, Gesellschaft Mit Beschrankter, Haftung, Penzig, Germany	1901	Burned
NIGHT DRIVERS FRIEND	Roberts & Mathews Ansonia, Ohio	1905	Stamped
EVENING STAR.	Edward Rorke & Co., New York, N.Y.	1877	Blown
PINTSCH	Safety Car Heating & Lighting Co., New York, N.Y.	1891	Blown, cut, or molded
PINTSCH			
SCRANTO	Scranton Acetylene Lamp Co., Scranton, Pa.	1911	Stamped
THE LITTLE BEAUTY	Silver & Co., New York, N.Y.	1889	Labels
TOM THUMB	Snell Cycle Fittings Co., Toledo, Ohio	1892	Engraved or painted
SEPULCHRE	Societe Anonyme Chauffage et Eclairage Sepulchre, of Herstal, Near Liege, Belgium	1879	Directly on goods or on a plate
Rayo	Standard Oil Co., Bayonne, N.J.	1906	Label

Trademark	Registrant	First used	The more permanent types of the mark
點 美 孚 油	Standard Oil Co. of New York, New York, N.Y.	1906	Etched
行孚美	Standard Oil Co. of New York, New York, N.Y.	1906	Embossed
 SOCONY	Standard Oil Co. of New York, New York, N.Y.	1908	Stamped
	Standard Oil Co. of New York, New York, N.Y.	1914	Stamped
S.Q.C.O. OF N.Y.	Standard Oil Co. of New York, New York, N.Y. Renewed to Socony-Vacuum Company	1914	Stamped
CYCLONE	Steam Gauge & Lantern Co., Syracuse, N.Y.	1891	Painted or stenciled
CALCITE	Steuben Glass Works, Corning, N.Y.	1910	Impressed
	Fr. Steüben & Co., Erfurt, Germany	1892	Impressed or stamped
	Sun Vapor Street Light Co., Canton, Ohio	1877	Stamped

Trademark	Registrant	First used	The more permanent types of the mark
SUN	Sun Vapor Street Light Co., Canton, Ohio	1877	"Applied to the goods"
KeroSafe	Thomas Manufacturing Co., Dayton, Ohio	1913	Label
Favrile fabrique	Tiffany Furnaces, Corona, N.Y.	1912	Label
WHICHWAY	J. W. Tobin, New York, N.Y.	1909	Stamped
LUSTRE	R. E. Tongue & Bros., Philadelphia, Pa.	1894	Ground
CARBONA	Walter Sinclair Traill, London, England	1902	Printed or stamped
20ᵗʰ CENTURY	20th Century M'F'G Co., New York, N.Y.	1901	Printed or stamped
Un-GRO-CO	United Grocers Co., Toledo, Ohio Assig. from C. C. Truax & Co.	1913	Label
THE ROCHESTER PAT. JAN. 15. 1884.	Charles S. Upton, New York, N.Y.	1884	Stamped
REFLEXOLIER	Welsbach Company, Gloucester City, N.J.	1908	Etched or stamped
MULTI-FLEX	Welsbach Company, Gloucester City, N.J.	1910	Etched or stamped
CORONA	Will & Baumer Co., Syracuse, N.Y.	1905	Label
HUB	George A. Young, Portland, Maine	1899	Embossed or frosted

GROUP III—Bottles and Jars

Trademark	Registrant	First used	The more permanent types of the mark
PRANA	Aerators Limited, London, England	1905	Blown
TONNEAU	Alart & McGuire, New York, N.Y.	1908	Blown
Icy-Hot	George P. Altenberg, Cincinnati, Ohio	1908	Embossed or etched
Ball	Ball Brothers Co., Muncie, Indiana and its predecessor, the Ball Brothers Glass Mfg. Co.	1894	"Molded." "Perfect" was added circa 1915
	L. A. Becker Co., Jersey City, N.J. and Chicago, Illinois	1908	Label
	Belle Vernon Mapes Dairy Co., Cleveland, Ohio	1914	Impressed
TIP TOP	Charles Boldt Glass Co., Cincinnati, Ohio	1904	Blown or stamped
	Bottlers Protective Assn., Baltimore, Maryland	1888	Blown
	M. S. Burr & Co., Boston, Mass. (Mfgr. of nursing bottles)	1874	Blown

Trademark	Registrant	First used	The more permanent types of the mark
MEDALLION	M. S. Burr & Co., Boston, Mass. (Mfgr. of nursing bottles)	1874	Blown
	M. S. Burr & Co., Boston, Mass. (Mfgr. of nursing bottles)	1874	Blown, or "in bas relief." Essential features are the eagle and "The Eagle Nursing Bottle."
SIGNET	Chicago Heights Bottle Co., Chicago Heights, Ill.	1913	Blown in the bottom
	Stanley S. Cline, Philadelphia, Pa.	1896	Label
MOUNT VERNON	Cook & Bernheimer Co., New York, N.Y.	1890	Blown or pressed
	William M. Decker, Kingston, N.Y.	1893	"Integrally formed," or on colored label
IDEAL	Hod C. Dunfee, Charleston, W.Va.	1910	Blown or molded
	Foley Bros. & Kelly Mercantile Co., St. Paul, Minn.	1897	Labels on jars, etc. for grocers' goods
LEOTRIC	John William Gayner, Salem, N.J.	1903	Imprinted
GLENSHAW	Glenshaw Glass Co., Glenshaw, Pa.	1904	Not specified
THE BEST	Gotham Co., New York, N.Y.	1891	Blown

Trademark	Registrant	First used	The more permanent types of the mark
G̶	Graham Glass Co., Evansville, Indiana Renewed to Owens-Illinois Glass Co., Toledo, Ohio.	1914	Imprinted
△ H	J. T. & A. Hamilton Co., Pittsburgh, Pa.	1900	Molded
OUR DARLING	W. H. Hamilton Co., Pittsburgh, Pa.	1899	"Affixed" to the bottle
ATLAS	Hazel-Atlas Glass Co., Wheeling, W.Va.	1902	Blown
GLOBE	Hemingray Glass Co., Covington, Ky. The symbol "Parquet-Lac" was used beginning 1895.	1886	Formed in the glass
ILLINOIS GLASS COMPANY BOTTLES OF EVERY DESCRIPTION	Illinois Glass Co., Alton, Illinois	1893	Label
◇ I ◇	Illinois Glass Co., Alton, Illinois	1915	Blown
BEAVER	Illinois-Pacific Glass Co., San Francisco, Calif. Fruit jars with a beaver design and name were made in Canada.	1910	Affixed to bottles and flasks
NP	Imperial Trust for the Encouragement of Scientific and Industrial Research, London, England	1907	Engraved
ˮBRILLIANTINEˮ	Jefferis Glass Co., Philadelphia, Pa.	1896	Blown
	Edward Kavalier of Neu Sazawa, Austria-Hungary	1910	Etched

Trademark	Registrant	First used	The more permanent types of the mark
	Kerr Glass Mfg. Corp., Sand Springs, Okla.	1903	Impressed or printed
"SELF SEALING"	Kerr Glass Mfg. Corp., Sand Springs, Okla.	1904	Printed
	Andrew Koch, New York, N.Y.	1875	Molded
KO—HI	Koehler & Hinrichs, St. Paul, Minnesota	1911	Impressed
	Albert Legrand, Manchester, N.H.	1898	Blown
	Wilbur F. Litch, Philadelphia, Pa.	1890	Marked on ink and mucilage bottles
VACO	John G. Lyman, White Plains, N.Y.	1907	Label
CALORIS	John G. Lyman, White Plains, N.Y.	1907	Label
COCA MARIANI	Mariani & Co., New York, N.Y.	1882	Blown on side and bottom
MARIANI-LIQUEUR	Mariani & Co., New York, N.Y.	1905	Blown in the body
Red ✠ Cross	Marion Flint Glass Co., Marion, Indiana	1894	Label

Trademark	Registrant	First used	The more permanent types of the mark
G UNION SEAL W	Henry Martin, Pittsburgh, Pa.	1883	Pressed or blown
S MAW SON & SONS LONDON ENGLAND	S. Maw, Son & Sons, London, England	1871	Marked on smelling-bottles and toilet articles
CRYSTO	McPike Drug Co., Kansas City, Missouri	1904	Blown
ON	Obear-Nester Glass Co., St. Louis, Missouri and East St. Louis, Illinois	1895	Molded
N	Obear-Nester Glass Co., St. Louis, Missouri and East St. Louis, Illinois	1895 (Reg. 1948)	Imprinted
	Obear-Nester Glass Co., St. Louis, Missouri and East St. Louis, Illinois	1896	Blown or cast in the bottom
	Obear-Nester Glass Co., St. Louis, Missouri and East St. Louis, Illinois	1899	Blown or cast in the bottom

Trademark	Registrant	First used	The more permanent types of the mark
	Obear-Nester Glass Co., St. Louis, Missouri and East St. Louis, Illinois	1900	Blown or cast in the bottom
	Pacific Coast Glass Works, San Francisco, Calif.	1913	Blown
	Philadelphia Vacuum Specialty Co., Philadelphia, Pa.	1911	Embossed or stamped on metal casing
Fredrop	Protective "Freflo" Stopple Co., Dover, Delaware, assignor from John W. Douglass	1914	Die-stamped or stenciled
LIGHTNING	Henry W. Putnam New York, N.Y.	1882 (Reg. 1927)	Pressed
	Quicksilver Mining Co., New Almaden, Calif.	1864	Painted
	L. Rose & Co. Limited, London, England	1874	Blown
	Schloss Crockery Co., San Francisco, Calif.	1910	"An integral part"

Trademark	Registrant	First used	The more permanent types of the mark
	Albert G. Smalley, Boston, Mass.	1891	Blown
WARRANTED FLASK	Albert G. Smalley, Boston, Mass.	1892	Blown
	Smalley, Kivlan & Onthank, Boston, Mass.	1910	Impressed
	Smalley, Kivlan & Onthank, Boston, Mass.	1914	Impressed
BLUE RIBBON	Standard Glass Co., Marion, Indiana	1908	Blown or molded
	C. Stolzles Sohne Actiengesellschaft fur Glasfabrikation, Vienna, Austria-Hungary	1905	Etched
O-U-KID	Robert A. Vancleave, Philadelphia, Pa.	1909	Blown
	Warren Fruit Jar Co., Fairfield, Iowa	1910	Blown
	T. C. Wheaton Co., Milville, N.J. The successor, the Wheaton Glass Co., used a W in a circle.	1903	Molded in the wall
MANHATTAN OVAL	Whitall, Tatum & Co. New York, N.Y.	1891	Blown or cast

Trademark	Registrant	First used	The more permanent types of the mark
FLINT-GREEN.	Whitney Glass Works, Glassborough, N.J.	1888	Blown
	Woodbury Glass Works, Woodbury, N.J. Essential features are "Woodbury" and the monogram "W G W."	1885	Blown
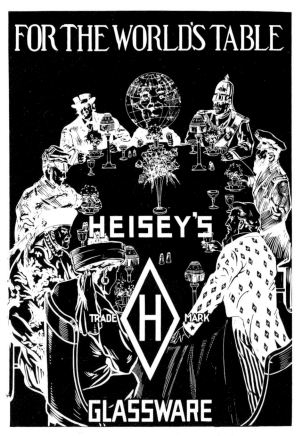	Charles J. Yost, Philadelphia, Pa.	1896	Label

FOR THE WORLD'S TABLE

HEISEY'S

TRADE MARK

GLASSWARE

Some Nonregistered Trademarks

Some firms have made little or no use of trademarks, whereas others used marks that never were registered. Some trademarks familiar to collectors were never registered in the Patent Office. Some better-known examples of these are:

A bee with **H** on the left wing, **I** on the body, and **G** on the right wing. The John B. Higbee Glass Co., Bridgeville, Pa. used this mark on various pieces of its Panelled Thistle and some other patterns, beginning 1907 and perhaps as late as 1916.

KRYS-TOL—This trademark name was coined by Benjamin W. Jacobs and used by the Ohio Flint Glass Co. in 1906-8; by the Jefferson Glass Co., 1908 to about 1918, and by the Central Glass Works, beginning 1919. (See HOBBIES Magazine, October 1967, p. 98N).

The Harry Northwood Glass Co., Wheeling, W.Va., according to Mrs. Kamm, began to use "the letter N, underscored, and inclosed or not," soon after acquiring an old glass house in Wheeling in 1902. The **N surrounded by two circles** was used until 1910, when, according to Sherman Hand in "Colors in Carnival Glass," it was replaced by a simplified mark—an **N in a small, raised circle**. Although Northwood used one or another of these marks on numerous items, much of his glassware was not marked.

A number of fruit-jar manufacturers used nonregistered trademarks, molded in the wall of the jars, in the early 1890s. Those observed in advertisements in *China, Glass and Lamps,* with the first year such advertisement was noted, are as follows:

DOME. Standard Glass Works, Wellsburg, W.Va.—1891. The glass lid was marked, "Pat. Aug. 7, 1883."

H F J Co. in a formee cross. Hero Fruit Jar Co., Philadelphia, Pa.—1892.

N in a shield. Nelson Glass Co., Muncie, Indiana—1893.

P in a shield. Standard Glass Works, Wellsburg, W.Va.—1892. and its successor, the S. George Co., Wellsburg, W.Va. —1893.

THE COLUMBIAN. Fairmount Bottle and Fruit Jar Co., Fairmount, W.Va.—1893. This unusual jar has a sealing lever to fit any of various notches on top of the glass lid. The neck has "several projections of solid glass for holding the neck band in position instead of the continuous flange on other jars, which necessarily weakens the neck."

The Sun Fruit Jar Co., 74 Wall Street, N.Y., N.Y. began advertising an interesting fruit jar in the *Crockery and Glass Journal* in 1900. On its wall is **"SUN TRADEMARK."** The word SUN is enclosed in a circle with rays to resemble the sun. This jar was alleged to be "The only perfectly hermetically sealed jar," with no metal to corrode and no wire to stretch.

Some Trademarks Introduced After 1914

Some of the glassware produced in the last few decades will be sought after by collectors of the next generation. Permanent markings such as that by the Westmoreland Glass Co. and the superimposed IG of the Imperial Glass Corporation will add to the interest and value of such glass.

Most American producers of colorful and artistic glassware have been averse to placing a permanent mark on their wares. Some contend that such marks mar the beauty and saleability, at least of clear glass, but the permanent trademarks placed on many Steuben and Heisey glasswares have added materially to their value.

Since the mid-1930's, various glass makers have featured a trademark with their name accompanied by a word or two to indicate some handwork in the production process, such as:

Blenko-Handcraft. Blenko Glass Co., Milton, W.Va., beginning 1934.

Bryce-Hand Blown. Bryce Brothers Co., Mt. Pleasant, Pa., beginning 1948.

Cambridge-Genuine Hand Made. Cambridge Glass Co., Cambridge, Ohio, beginning 1927.

Fenton-Authentic Handmade. Fenton Art Glass Co., Williamstown, W.Va., beginning 1950.

Rainbow-Hand Decorated, in a rainbow design. Rainbow Art Glass Co., Huntington, W.Va., beginning 1943. A later mark has **"Hand Blown by Rainbow,"** enclosed in a loop.

Unfortunately these trademarks apparently appear only on paper labels which tend to disappear with the first washing.

One or more letters in a circle or other enclosure has been a common type of trademark, especially on containers made in the last 50 years. Many permanent marks of this type may be observed on the bottom of bottles and jars on grocery-store shelves. A number of these marks (some of which have not been registered), along with the registrant and year of first use are as follows:

A in a circle. Armstrong Cork Co., Lancaster, Pa.—1938.

A H K—A. H. Kerr & Co., Los Angeles, Calif.—1944. The word Kerr was used as a trademark beginning 1915.

A W in an oval. American-Wheaton Glass Corp., Milville, N.J.—1961.

B, B in a circle, or **B in three concentric circles.** Brockway Glass Co., Brockway, Pa.—1925.

B-C in two incomplete, contiguous circles. Bartlett-Collins Co., Sapulpa, Okla.—1932.

C in two concentric circles (some with a bottle design superimposed at an angle). Chattanooga Glass Co., Chattanooga, Tenn.—1927.

C in a triangle with rounded corners. Consumers Glass Co., Montreal and Toronto, Canada.

C in a rectangle. Crystal Glass Co., Los Angeles, Calif.—1921.

D within two horizontal diamonds. Dominion Glass Co., Montreal, Canada.

F in a shield. Federal Glass Co., Columbus, Ohio—1932.

F in a hexagon. Fairmount Glass Works, Indianapolis, Ind.—1933.

F F in script in a circle. Foster-Forbes Glass Co., Marion, Ind.—1942.

G in a circle. Gulfport Glass Corp., Gulfport, Miss.—1954.

G and C overlapping, bordered by triangles and enclosed in a rectangle. Glass Containers, Inc., Los Angeles, Calif.—1933.

H superimposed on a ship anchor. Anchor Hocking Glass Corp., Lancaster, Ohio—1938.

H straddling an A, in a circle. Hazel Atlas Glass Corp., Wheeling, W.Va. —1923.

I and G superimposed. The I has curved ends and a dot at the top. Imperial Glass Corp., Bellaire, Ohio—1951.

I and G superimposed. Iroquois Glass Industries, Candiac, P.Q., Canada.

J in a square. Jeannette Glass Co., Jeannette, Pa.—1940.

K. John E. Kemple Glass Works, Kenova, W.Va.

K above a six-sided polygon. Kimble Glass Co., Vineland, N.J.—1920. The **K inside the six-sided polygon** was first used in 1936.

K in a Keystone. Knox Glass, Inc., Knox, Pa.—1932.

L (in script) in a three-segment circle. Libbey Glass Division, Owens-Illinois, Toledo, Ohio—1937. Discontinued.

L in a circle. Libbey Glass Division, Owens-Illinois, Toledo, Ohio. On drinking glasses and sherbet dishes—1955; on tableware and glass kitchenware—1963.

L in a square. Lincoln Container Corp., Lincoln, Illinois.

L G. Liberty Glass Co., Sapulpa, Oklahoma—1953. **L-G** (an odd G)— 1936.

M in a circle. Maryland Glass Corp., Baltimore, in the bottom of its colorful bottles—1921.

M in a six-sided polygon. Metro Glass Co., Jersey City, N.J.

O in a square. Owens Bottle Co., Toledo, Ohio—1919.

O and G, superimposed and inclosed in a circle. Olean Glass Co., Olean, N.Y.—1929.

O around I. Owens-Illinois, Toledo, Ohio—1954. This mark, with a superimposed diamond was first used in 1929.

P in a circle. Pierce Glass Co., Port Allegany, Pa.

P and C in complementary quadrangles. Pacific Coast Glass Works, San Francisco, Calif.—1919.

T M C in a monogram. Thatcher Glass Mfg. Co., Elmira, N.Y.—1923.

U and G superimposed, or **U G P.** Universal Glass Products Co., Parkersburg, W.Va.

W in a circle. Wheaton Glass Co., Milville, N.J.

W above T, surrounded by a triangle. Whitall, Tatum & Co., Milville, N.J.—1924.

The "Index of Registrants," maintained in the Patent Office, for the period January 1, 1931 to date, indicates that some of the large glass companies registered many trademarks from 1931 to 1967. Many of these, however, were not for use on glassware.

British Registry Marks 1842 – 1883

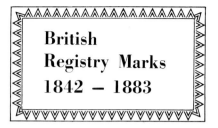

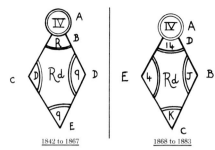

1842 to 1867   1868 to 1883

The original purpose of the Registry Mark was to protect manufacturers from having their designs pirated by competitors, for much the same reason present day inventions are copyrighted.

The protection was given for an initial period of three years after the manufacturer had filed his design with the British Patent Office. After he had made his filing, the manufacturer was entitled to mark his wares by printing or impressing them with the diamond shaped device.

As a rule of thumb, if the mark is *printed* it applies to the decoration, but if it is *impressed* into the material then it relates to the shape of the object.

It should be remembered that the registry date does not necessarily mean that the piece was *made* on that date, but merely the date when the design or bundle was filed. A popular design or shape could be produced for some time after its original introduction and still carry the same mark.

The registering of marks was not limited to British manufacturers, though they made up the majority. Some designs were registered by foreign manufacturers or their agents, so it can readily be seen that the existence of the mark is not infallible evidence that the item was of British origin.

The manufacturer sometimes applied his name, either with an impressed mark or in some other way, in addition to the Registry Mark. In that case, identification was complete.

The Registry Mark for both periods (1842-1867 and 1868-1883) was basically the same format—a long shaped diamond surmounted by a circle intersecting the upper acute angle, the letters "Rd" in the center, and other letters or numerals in the remaining angles. (See illustration.)

The key to both Registry Marks is as follows:

A . . . . . Class. (I for metal, II for wood, III for glass, and IV for ceramic ware.)
B . . . . . Year.
C . . . . . Month.
D . . . . . Day.
E . . . . Bundle, or parcel number.

1842 - 1867 YEAR INDEX

X	1842	E	1855
H	1843	L	1856
C	1844	K	1857
A	1845	B	1858
I	1846	M	1859
F	1847	Z	1860
U	1848	R	1861
S	1849	O	1862
V	1850	G	1863
P	1851	N	1864
D	1852	W	1865
Y	1853	Q	1866
J	1854	T	1867

1868 - 1883 YEAR INDEX

X	1868	V	1876
H	1869	P	1877
C	1870	D	1878
A	1871	Y	1879
I	1872	J	1880
F	1873	E	1881
U	1874	L	1882
S	1875	K	1883

INDEX TO MONTHS (APPLIES TO *BOTH* PERIODS)

C	January	I	July
G	February	R	August
W	March	D	September
H	April	B	October
E	May	K	November
M	June	A	December

Deciphering the mark is complicated as certain errors in allotment occurred:

For September 1857, the letter R (belonging to August) was used.

For December 1860, the letter K (belonging to November) was used.

Between March 1 and March 6, 1878, Registry Marks with the letter W for the year were sent out. However, this need not confuse anybody translating a mark, because this W is in the angle at the right, where D ought to be. It will be the only case where a letter W occurs in the angle at the right, for the table of year letters of the second mark contains no W.

In determining whether a Registry Mark was in the first or second period, look at the device in the compartment directly under the circle at the top of the diamond. If a letter is there it indicates the first mark; if a figure, the article is of the second period.

Reproduced from the WESTERN COLLECTOR, July 1966, by permission of the publisher.

AN INDEX*TO
"400 TRADEMARKS ON GLASS"

Word and letter marks are listed with initial caps, whereas descriptions of marks are all in small letters.

* Index compiled by Robert A. Elder, Jr. and supplemented by the author.

A trademark may become so successful as to prove its failure. If a trademark becomes so completely identified with a product as to become its common or generic name, the legal rights in the name as a trademark have been destroyed. Examples of this are aspirin, cellophane, linoleum and milk of magnesia.